BETHLEHEM, THE YEAR JESUS WAS BORN

THE STORY OF CHRISTMAS FOR TEENS

SCOTT DOUGLAS

CONTENTS

Introduction	7
1. THE INCARNATION?	11
2. THE BIG B-DAY	15
JESUS' BIRTHDAY?	16
WHAT IS WINTER SOLSTICE?	17
3. THE HOLY LIST	19
4. THE VIRGIN BIRTH?	25
THE BASICS OF VIRGINITY	26
THE ELEPHANT IN THE ROOM	27
5. MARY AND JOSEPH	31
JOSEPH: A MAN OF FEW WORDS	32
MARY: THE MOTHER WHO KNEW BEST	39
RAISING A CHILD OF GOD	42
6. OTHER CHARACTERS	45
SIMEON: THE MAN WHO WAITED FOR GOD'S PROMISE	46
ANNA: THE FAITHFUL WOMAN WITH AN UNYIELDING HEART	47
HEROD: THE "GREAT" VILLAIN OF THE CHRISTMAS STORY	48

ZECHARIAH: THE PRIESTLY FATHER	49
THE HEAVENLY MESSENGER	50
7. THE TOWN OF BETHLEHEM	53
HISTORICAL BETHLEHEM	53
BETHLEHEM AT THE TIME OF JESUS' BIRTH	54
THE INN	55
THE MANGER	56
A HUMBLE DELIVERY ROOM FIT FOR A KING	57
FROM BETHLEHEM TO EGYPT: PARALLELS WITH MOSES	58
8. STAR OF BETHLEHEM	61
THE BIBLICAL STAR	61
THE SCIENTIFIC STAR	62
CHRISTMAS LIGHTS: A MODERN STAR	63
9. THE SHEPHERDS	67
THE BIBLICAL SHEPHERDS	68
WHO WERE THE SHEPHERDS?	69
THE SHEPHERDS' MESSAGE	70
10. THE WISE MEN	73
THE BIBLICAL ACCOUNT OF THE WISE MEN	74
WHO WERE THE WISE MEN?	75
WHAT DO THE WISE MEN REPRESENT?	76
WHY THE WISE MEN?	77
WHAT DOES IT MEAN THAT THEY WORSHIPED?	79

WHAT HAPPENED TO THE
WISE MEN? 79
MORE THAN MEETS
THE EYE? 80

11. THE GIFTS 83
    Epilogue 87

    Appendix A: Advent 91
    Appendix B: History of Christmas 95

INTRODUCTION

I'm twelve, and it's 1988. For days, I've been eyeing this huge box under our Christmas tree. It's wrapped and tagged:

From Santa; To Cookie

Cookie is our beagle—sometimes obedient, always loved. My brother and I can't stop talking about that box. Why would Santa bring something this big for our dog? Why was it here early? The suspense is real.

Christmas morning finally arrives. Cookie doesn't care about the mystery box; she's too busy gnawing on a huge bone my parents gave her. So, naturally, my brother and I take over, ripping off the paper in the classic Christmas chaos. And there it is:

A Nintendo system, complete with the Power Pad and *World Class Track Meet.*

It turns out my parents tricked us by labeling the gift for Cookie so we wouldn't guess. Smart, right? And maybe, just maybe, you've had your own Christmas surprise that felt like magic. Whether it was something handmade or the gift you'd been hoping for all year, we all have those memories—some good, some weird, and some unforgettable.

Most people know what Christmas is all about—but let's be honest, the gifts play a huge role. I'm not here to guilt-trip you about that or tell you to replace presents with a volunteer shift at a soup kitchen (though, hey, do that if you feel called!). Gifts are part of the Christmas tradition for a reason, and there's nothing wrong with enjoying that.

This book isn't here to say, "Give up on Christmas fun." It's here to explore what Christmas really means. Sure, we know the story—even people who don't celebrate it know about the Nativity, the Wise Men, and their gifts. But if we're honest, the story can feel a little flat, almost like a fairy tale.

But what if it's way more than that? What if

Introduction 9

each piece, each gift, and each scene holds a message—a part of God's gift to us that we're meant to unwrap slowly, like an endless Christmas present?

Imagine this: Would it matter if Jesus was born in Rome instead of Bethlehem, or if one of the Wise Men brought a pizza instead of frankincense? Probably not. Yet every detail is there for a reason. Over the centuries, cultures have added their own twists and traditions, and that's cool too. But beneath it all, there's a deeper, original story—a message meant just for us.

So, let's dig in. Let's see beyond the wrapping paper and discover why Christmas is more than decorations, pageants, and a Nativity set. It's about a gift with layers and meaning, a story God wrapped up and placed under the tree of history for us to discover.

This is the story of Christmas: God's greatest gift, and it's waiting for you to open.

1

THE INCARNATION?

If you want to understand Christmas, you'd probably look to the Bible first, right? That's where most of the story we know is. But here's something unexpected: in two of the gospels—Mark and John—you won't find anything about Jesus' birth. That's right. Mark, thought to be the first gospel writer, and John, likely the last, didn't even mention it.

Weird, right? I mean, a virgin birth is a pretty big deal. Imagine someone you know claiming to be born from a virgin—aside from that odd guy who sometimes tries to recruit people outside Walmart, you probably don't know anyone like that. So why didn't Mark and John think it was important to include?

There are some theories. For one, each writer had a unique audience. Mark was trying to reach Romans, so he kept things short and to the point, focusing on what would grab them. Jesus' family history might not have been that compelling to them. John, on the other hand, was all about big ideas and philosophy. He was trying to dive deep into the meaning behind Jesus' life, not just the events themselves.

John even writes in 20:30 that "Jesus did many other things that aren't recorded in this book." In other words, we're not getting the full story—there are probably plenty of "deleted scenes" that didn't make it into the final cut. The point is, people weren't following Jesus just for his miracles but for what he represented, what he was teaching. So, while miracles were part of the story, the authors wanted to make sure they highlighted the meaning behind them.

This brings us to the real theme: the incarnation. The story of Jesus' birth isn't just about a miracle; it's about what that miracle symbolizes. Matthew and Luke—unlike Mark and John—include the birth story for a reason. Sure, a virgin birth is fascinating, but does it really matter to our faith?

Turns out, it kind of does. Without the virgin birth, some of the theology behind Christmas and Christianity falls apart. Think about it: Jesus being born from a virgin is more than just a cool plot twist. It's tied to the idea that Jesus was both fully human and fully divine—what Christians call the incarnation.

Here's the idea behind it:

1. Jesus is divine.

2. Jesus is human.

3. Jesus is both of these things at once—two natures in one person.

But why did God go with this plan? Why not just send a prophet or show up as a fully divine being? Here's the thing: God didn't need to prove he existed. Faith doesn't need proof. But by becoming human, he showed us that he truly understood what it's like to live in our world, to feel our pain and challenges.

Even though John skips the Christmas story, he gives us a hint in John 1:14: "The Word became flesh." That's basically saying, "God came out of the words on a page and showed up in person." God became human to let us know he's close to us, that he understands what we go through, and that he's with us.

So when we think about the virgin birth within this bigger picture, it all connects. Christmas isn't just about a miraculous birth— it's about a miracle that started the journey of God being with us, understanding us, and showing that there's no separation between him and us anymore.

For Matthew, who was writing to people who knew about the separation between God and humanity, and for Luke, who wanted to tell the most accurate story he could, this was a detail they couldn't leave out. It was the start of something that would change everything.

2

THE BIG B-DAY

Before we jump into the Christmas story itself, let's take a little detour to think about the holiday itself. But right now, let's focus on something a bit surprising—the actual date of Christmas.

I don't think this will come as a shock, but December 25th probably isn't Jesus' birthday. Most people know this, but if you didn't—sorry to break it to you! Jesus wouldn't be getting a free stack of birthday pancakes at IHOP on Christmas morning.

December 25th is simply the day we've chosen to celebrate. Does it matter? Is there any meaning behind that date itself?

While the date isn't exactly rooted in the

Bible, it does have a unique history that's worth exploring before we get into what the Bible actually says about Christmas.

JESUS' BIRTHDAY?

I still remember the first time someone told me Jesus wasn't born on December 25. It was a kid around Christmas who thought this "discovery" meant that Jesus couldn't possibly exist. Their reasoning was basically, "If people lied about this date, then maybe they lied about everything else too." At the time, it sounded kind of convincing, but now I see how it doesn't really hold up.

It's fair to wonder, though, why we celebrate on December 25 if no one knows Jesus' actual birthday. Why not pick a summer day or even January 1 for a New Year's and Christmas combo?

The date of December 25 was officially chosen around 400 AD by Pope Julius. Yes, there were pagan holidays around that time of year, but the decision wasn't just about converting people. It was about meeting people where they were. The church essentially said,

"You're already celebrating something, so let's keep the spirit of celebration but focus on Jesus." Not long after, around 480 AD, Christians began using the term "Advent," meaning "coming," to mark the season leading up to Christmas.

WHAT IS WINTER SOLSTICE?

You've probably heard people say that Christmas is really just a renamed pagan holiday. They're probably referring to Winter Solstice, which falls around December 21 or 22. But if you ask them what Winter Solstice is, they might not fully know.

The word "solstice" comes from two Latin words: *sol* (sun) and *sistere* (to stand still). Basically, it's the day when the sun "stands still," marking the longest night of the year. For ancient cultures, it symbolized the end of the darkest days and the promise of spring.

While gods were honored during the Solstice, each culture had its own take. For example, the Romans celebrated Saturn, the god of agriculture. In Germany, people honored Odin. And, yes, there was a god, Sol

Invictus, whose celebration fell on December 25. But not everyone was focused on gods— many were just glad that the hard winter was ending and that better days were coming. It was a bit like their version of New Year's.

So, when the early Christian leaders set December 25 as the date for Christmas, it wasn't some sneaky scheme to erase other traditions. They chose it to make it easier for people to celebrate without feeling like they had to completely change their culture. The goal was to bring the meaning of Christmas into existing traditions, not to replace or erase them.

3

THE HOLY LIST

We all know that one relative. The one who says things that make everyone cringe. The one with the wild stories or controversial opinions who keeps everyone just a little on edge. Maybe you even are that relative!

Picture a holiday gathering. Everyone's chatting, it's cozy, and then someone says something that instantly raises eyebrows. That's the family member I'm talking about. And no matter how much we might wish we could avoid them, family connections are strong. They're with us for life, even if we try to cut ties or ignore them.

I had a few of those family members

growing up. I remember sitting at the kids' table, and some uncle would drift over to share tales that were totally boring or just plain awkward for a kid. One uncle would tell wild, inappropriate stories about his adventures in New Orleans during Mardi Gras. I didn't get most of it back then, and now, as an adult, it's just embarrassing to remember!

Family history has its own "black sheep" stories—the stuff no one talks about but everyone knows. One family member wasn't allowed at gatherings because of a dark rumor, which split the family's opinions. As a kid, I didn't know the details, but I was warned to stay away. The one time he did show up, the entire family's reaction was so intense that it felt like people were reliving old traumas. I couldn't understand why everyone pretended like nothing happened for so long.

Unfortunately, most families have that kind of pain. But no matter what, family is family. We're connected to them by blood, even if they're not in our lives anymore.

But how does this relate to the Christmas story?

Back in Jesus' time, family was more than

just the people you saw at reunions. It defined your status. People thought of you as the product of your family. That's why people were so shocked to hear Jesus teaching—they said, "Wait, isn't he the carpenter's son?" Meaning, how could he possibly be more than what his family's status allowed?

The Bible gives us two family trees for Jesus: one in Matthew and one in Luke. Mark and John skip Jesus' early life entirely because their audiences didn't need it. But Matthew and Luke include Jesus' genealogy to show his connection to King David, emphasizing that Jesus came from a respected family line. This was important to prove that Jesus wasn't just a myth or legend; he was real, with real ancestors.

Here's where things get interesting: Matthew's genealogy includes some serious "black sheep." And not only that—it includes women, which was unheard of at the time. Typically, family histories only mentioned men. But Matthew lists five women. That might not seem like a big deal today, but 2,000 years ago, this was huge! Even more shocking, some of these women weren't even Jewish.

Including them would've been like listing the family's "secrets" for everyone to see.

And if that's not enough, these women had messy, complicated stories. Tamar tricked her father-in-law into having a child with her. Rahab was a well-known prostitute—and she wasn't even Jewish; she was a Canaanite. Each of these women had what you might call an "unconventional" life. But they also took control of their situations and made bold choices. They weren't defined by the messiness of their pasts.

So, to a Jewish reader of Matthew's genealogy, these names would have stood out. They would've thought, "This family history is a mess!" These were outsiders, people with complicated pasts. And it raises a pretty big question: why would Matthew include people with such questionable backgrounds in the family line of Jesus?

The answer is powerful: Jesus didn't come just for the powerful or the "perfect" people. He came for everyone—the outcasts, the misunderstood, the flawed. He came for people with real struggles, people who'd been through difficult situations, people who needed hope.

The true story of Christmas isn't about family gatherings, self-improvement, or reflections on the past year. Yes, those things are part of it. But Christmas is about one central truth: God's love for us, shown by giving us a Savior.

And the genealogy of Jesus is a reminder that families can be complicated. The Bible doesn't ignore the rough spots or pretend they don't exist. God doesn't say, "Pretend nothing happened" or "Forget what went wrong." Instead, he shows us that he can work through even the darkest moments in our family history. Jesus' family line had its own share of drama and hardship, yet out of that lineage came the ultimate story of redemption. It's a story that reminds us God loves us as we are—flaws and all. And he can use even the difficult parts of our lives for good.

4

THE VIRGIN BIRTH?

We can't really dig into the real meaning of Christmas without touching on a topic people rarely bring up around the holidays—sex. Yep, you read that right. If you're blushing at the thought of the "s-word" in a Christmas book, feel free to swap it out with something like "frickle-frackle" as you read on.

Depending on how you grew up, Mary's virginity might be no big deal, or it might be central to everything you believe about Christmas—second only to the resurrection of Christ. But no matter your background, you probably assume Mary was a virgin. But why does it matter so much?

And while you're thinking about her virginity, let's break down what that word even means. Was she simply a "pure young woman"? Did she remain a virgin her whole life, or did she only stay a virgin until after Jesus' birth? And what about Joseph? Could Mary have married anyone else and still brought Jesus into the world the same way?

Turns out, the virginity of Mary isn't quite as straightforward as we're taught in Sunday school.

THE BASICS OF VIRGINITY

So, assuming Mary was a virgin, why is this important? There are three main reasons:

1. **Jesus Isn't Man-Made:** If Joseph were Jesus' biological father, then Jesus would be fully human with no divine nature. But if Mary was a virgin, then Jesus is a mix—half man, half divine.
2. **Sinless Birth:** According to some theology, people inherit sin from

their fathers. With a virgin birth, Jesus skips this inheritance, so he's born sinless.

3. **Perfect Sacrifice:** Back then, sacrifices had to be pure and spotless. Since Jesus was sinless, he was considered the ultimate "perfect" sacrifice, the only one who could offer himself for humanity.

We'll get into why Mary had to marry Joseph (and not, say, Joe the Plumber) in the next chapter. But for now, we can understand that when we say Mary was a "virgin," we're talking about it in the traditional sense—she hadn't had sex. And while some people debate if she remained a virgin her entire life, we'll keep it simple for this Christmas discussion.

THE ELEPHANT IN THE ROOM

Here's the big question: if the virgin birth is so important, why don't John, Mark, and the epistles talk about it?

It's not that they deny the virgin birth; they

just don't mention it. Why? Audience. The readers of John and Mark were likely familiar with the virgin birth, so there wasn't a need to cover it. Their focus was on Jesus' life and ministry, not his birth.

Still, John gives us a hint. In John 8:41, the Jews say, "'We're not illegitimate children. The only Father we have is God himself.'" In other words, people knew that there was something unique about Jesus' birth—almost like a "family secret."

Now, in Matthew's account, he wants to be crystal clear that Jesus' birth wasn't the result of adultery. He's out to squash any rumors that Mary had cheated on Joseph. Meanwhile, Luke's account shines the spotlight on Mary and is more female-centered. Joseph is more of a side character, and we don't get his reactions or even an angel explaining things to him. Luke emphasizes the role women played in the Nativity story.

In contrast, Matthew gives Joseph a bigger role. He's all about showing where Jesus fits into history, establishing his genealogy and connection to King David. Matthew's main

Bethlehem, the Year Jesus Was Born

theme is that Jesus is the "new Moses"—the start of a new covenant. And that covenant begins with the virgin birth. Without it, the whole story would look different.

5

MARY AND JOSEPH

We've spent the last few chapters diving deep into theology—hope it's been as thrilling as a holiday thrill ride! But Christmas isn't just about theological ideas; it's also about real people. So, before we go any further, let's talk about the two most familiar faces in the Christmas story: Joseph and Mary.

You probably know their story well—maybe you've even played one of them in a Christmas pageant. Mary, the pure and innocent virgin; Joseph, the faithful and loyal husband who sticks by her. But that's only scratching the surface—there's a lot more to these two than we usually think about.

Just like our own families influence us, Mary and Joseph shaped Jesus in big ways. Yes, Jesus was part human, so while his divine nature was unchangeable, his human nature was shaped by the values and example of his earthly parents. Who knows? With different influences, maybe Jesus could have ended up as an influential figure in Rome rather than on the cross.

So, what can we learn about Joseph and Mary that would have influenced Jesus?

JOSEPH: A MAN OF FEW WORDS

For a long time, people have had some creative ideas about who Joseph was—many believe he was an older widower with kids from a previous marriage. But none of that is actually in the Bible. So where did these ideas come from?

Around 150 AD, a book called the *Gospel of James* was written to answer some questions early Christians had about Joseph. This book —also known as the *Protoevangelium of James*— wasn't part of the Bible, but it offered "solutions" for things that puzzled early believers.

Here were the main "problems" people had with Joseph:

1. The Bible says Jesus had brothers and sisters.
2. Jesus is called both the Son of God and the son of Joseph.

Some early Christians didn't like the idea of Mary having other children, so this extra-biblical gospel suggested Joseph already had kids from a previous marriage, making Mary a perpetual virgin. It also made Joseph a very old widower—90 years old!—who married a young Mary and cared for her in a totally non-romantic way. And, according to this story, he even died at age III.

While this made for some creative back-story, none of it is in the Bible. So let's take a look at the Joseph we actually see in Scripture.

THE BIBLICAL JOSEPH

The Bible gives us only a few glimpses of Joseph, mainly in the gospels of Matthew and Luke. Mark and John mention him briefly as Jesus' father, but that's about it.

In Matthew 1:18-19, we learn that Joseph

was engaged to Mary and discovers that she's pregnant before they've been together. At first, he assumes she's been unfaithful, but, being a good guy, he decides to divorce her quietly so she won't be disgraced. Matthew even calls him a "righteous man," emphasizing that he followed Jewish law and wanted to do the right thing.

But then, in Matthew 1:20, an angel appears to Joseph in a dream, explaining that Mary's child is from the Holy Spirit. After that, Joseph is all in—he stays with Mary and becomes the earthly father to Jesus.

Both Matthew and Luke tell us that Joseph was descended from King David, which is important for fulfilling prophecy about the Messiah. And we know that Joseph was a carpenter (or craftsman, as the original word could mean). He had a humble, working-class job, and his sons would have been expected to follow in his footsteps rather than pursuing higher status roles like philosophers.

We also know Joseph wasn't wealthy. In Luke 2:24, we see him sacrificing two pigeons at the temple, which was the offering required of those who couldn't afford a lamb. And Luke

1:42 mentions that Joseph and Mary made a yearly trip to Jerusalem for Passover, which implies they stayed together and continued their family life.

After these stories, Joseph disappears from the narrative. Most believe he likely passed away before Jesus began his public ministry.

That's about it for Joseph in the Bible—no mention of him being 90 years old, no tales of him living to be 111, and nothing about him never having kids with Mary. The Bible simply portrays him as a kind, faithful, and humble man who did his best to raise the Son of God in his own quiet way.

THE JOSEPH THAT JESUS KNEW

Joseph remains a bit of a mystery. We only know a few details about him, but from these, we get a glimpse of why God might have chosen him to raise his only son. Imagine being in Joseph's position: you're about to marry, everything seems to be falling into place, and then Mary tells you she's pregnant —with God's child.

What would you do?

The Bible doesn't go into Joseph's thoughts, but we can imagine he felt shock, betrayal, anger, maybe even all of these at once. Joseph had a few options:

1. Publicly accuse Mary, which would not only shame her but also return his dowry, giving him a financial reset.
2. Quietly divorce her and move on.
3. Stay with her and raise the child as his own.

The Bible tells us that Joseph was a "righteous man," meaning he followed Jewish law and tradition. It would have been easy for him to take a path that upheld his reputation and honored tradition. But the one emotion we do know he felt was compassion. Even before he understood the divine nature of the situation, Joseph chose the option with the least harm for Mary—quietly ending things to spare her any public disgrace.

Jesus' teachings are full of compassion, and while we often think of these as divine traits, some of this compassion might well have come from his earthly father's example. Joseph demonstrated compassion at a moment when he didn't have to, showing us that even small choices can have a lasting impact.

Just as Joseph decides on this quiet divorce, an angel appears in his dream, calling him "Son of David"—a term only Jesus is later associated with. This title links Joseph to the royal lineage of David, underscoring Jesus' rightful claim to this heritage. The angel's message appeals to both Joseph's pride in his lineage and his faith, urging him to trust that Mary's child will fulfill scripture.

Even after hearing this divine confirmation, Joseph knew the consequences of staying with Mary. He understood how society would view an unwed couple with a child. Their reputation would likely be affected for life. Yet Joseph stayed, accepting the cost of judgment from others, and this experience could have influenced Jesus' later compassion toward women judged by society.

Joseph's faith and obedience didn't end there. Shortly after Jesus' birth, he has another dream where he's instructed to flee with Mary and the baby to Egypt. This wasn't a quick or easy journey—over 300 miles across difficult terrain. But Joseph trusted God's message and protected his family, teaching Jesus a powerful lesson in faithfulness.

If there's one word to describe Joseph, it's "faithful." He lived a life that taught Jesus by example. Joseph wasn't wealthy; when they went to the temple, he offered pigeons, which was a sacrifice only the poor made. Growing up in a modest household likely shaped Jesus' perspective on wealth, setting the foundation for his teachings on a life without material excess.

After the temple visit when Jesus was twelve, Joseph disappears from the narrative, leading most to believe he passed away young. This may have been Jesus' first real experience of loss, something that deeply shaped his understanding of human suffering.

My grandfather was a man of few words, a World War II vet who rarely spoke about his experiences. Yet, I learned so much from him —not through what he said, but through his actions. I think Joseph was like that for Jesus. Joseph didn't have to give long speeches or provide philosophical teachings; he simply lived a faithful, humble life that taught Jesus how to live as a man.

In storytelling, there's a saying: "show, don't tell." Readers want to see action and draw conclusions themselves, rather than being told how to feel. Joseph seems to have shown Jesus through his actions, a lesson that Jesus would carry into his own ministry. When people asked questions, Jesus didn't just give answers; he told parables. Like Joseph, he taught by showing, not just telling.

MARY: THE MOTHER WHO KNEW BEST

Mary, like Joseph, is surrounded by stories and legends. Many of these have become cherished traditions in certain churches. For instance, Catholics believe Mary was assumed into heaven rather than experiencing death, and some say she remained a lifelong virgin. In Islam, Mary is also revered as one of history's greatest women.

But fortunately, we don't need legends to understand Mary's role—just the biblical account.

THE BIBLICAL MARY

So, what do we really know about Mary from the Bible? Not a lot, actually. Based on cultural norms of the time, Mary was likely between 14 and 20 when she became engaged to Joseph. After hearing from the angel that she would bear a child by the Holy Spirit, her initial reaction is one of confusion, "How can this be?" (Luke 1:34).

Mary's journey shows a realistic version of faith—one that allows for questions and doubts. Faith doesn't necessarily mean having all the answers; it's about choosing to trust even when you don't fully understand. Mary's obedience isn't about instant certainty but about taking a leap of faith and trusting God step by step.

While some traditions portray Mary as sinless, the Bible doesn't suggest this. In Luke 1:47, Mary calls God "my Savior," implying she, too, needed saving from sin.

The Bible shows that Mary was present at key moments in Jesus' life—at the Wedding at Cana (John 2:1-11), urging him to act when the wine ran out; at the cross (John 19:25-27); and in the upper room with the disciples after his ascension (Acts 1:14). Though she's not frequently mentioned, these moments hint

Bethlehem, the Year Jesus Was Born

that she was a respected part of Jesus' inner circle.

THE MARY JESUS KNEW

Think back to yourself at sixteen. Even if you weren't rebellious, you likely weren't quite ready for the responsibilities of adulthood. But Mary, at a young age, was thrust into an incredibly difficult situation. She was engaged to a humble carpenter, at the bottom of the social ladder, and suddenly, she was pregnant by unconventional means. She accepted it with maturity and faith beyond her years.

For nine months, Mary carried not only a child but the weight of societal judgment and whispers. It's likely she had moments of doubt. And when Jesus later ventured into the wilderness, he might have remembered Mary's quiet strength—the lesson that faith doesn't eliminate doubt but grows alongside it, building resilience.

We don't know all of what Mary taught Jesus, but it's easy to imagine she had some heart-to-heart talks with him—not "the talk," but conversations about making tough choices and putting God above everything. Mary's life was a testament to making those hard choices, as she endured years of stares and whispers in her community. While we celebrate Mary as a saint today, her contemporaries may not have viewed her that way. She knew she had done the right thing, but living with the consequences couldn't have been easy.

And maybe, when Jesus prayed in the Garden of Gethsemane, wrestling with the weight of his mission, he thought of Mary. He might have drawn on the memory of his mother, someone who intimately understood the cost of doing God's will. Just as Mary had accepted the challenges that came with God's plan, Jesus also chose to "take the cup" in obedience (Matthew 26:39; Mark 14:36).

In Mary, Jesus had a living example of faith, courage, and obedience, even when God's will came with human hardships. It was a home where God's blessing didn't necessarily mean an easy path but one that ultimately fulfilled a divine purpose.

RAISING A CHILD OF GOD

Every child around us is shaped by the people in their lives. While parents hold the main responsibility, all of us—uncles, aunts, grandparents, cousins, neighbors—play a part in influencing them. We each have a role in passing down the kind of values that Mary and Joseph did, teaching through our actions and words.

When we look at Jesus, it's easy to think he turned out as he did because he was God. But that's only part of it. Jesus became who he was not just because of his divine nature, but because he had parents who taught him real-life lessons—the very foundation he later built his ministry upon.

Christmas is a time to pause and look at the children in our lives with fresh eyes. Think of Jesus and the people who influenced him. Reflect on your actions and how you can be a living example, showing—not just telling—the lessons that will stay with these young ones as they grow.

6

OTHER CHARACTERS

Mary and Joseph might be the main players in the Nativity story, but they're backed by a unique ensemble of characters that add depth and richness to the Christmas narrative. Without them, Christmas just wouldn't feel complete. This chapter will introduce those lesser-known figures who briefly appear but play essential roles.

(We'll save the Wise Men and Shepherds for their own chapter since they're an ensemble in their own right.)

SIMEON: THE MAN WHO WAITED FOR GOD'S PROMISE

Every character in the Bible has a purpose, a lesson to teach. Simeon may seem like a minor character, but his presence holds significance. He's introduced as an elderly man who had been promised by the Holy Spirit that he would live to see the Messiah. Simeon spent his life in patient waiting, trusting God's word despite the years passing by.

Simeon's life teaches us about patience and faith. He spent years hoping for something he had no control over, trusting that God's promise would come true in its own time. And when he finally saw Jesus, he didn't just see a baby—he saw the Messiah. Simeon's faith reveals that God's timing may not match our own, but it's always worth the wait.

He also has another purpose in the story. When Simeon sees Jesus, he recognizes Mary's role, telling her that she's not just the mother of a child but the mother of the Messiah. Simeon's words help Mary understand her own place in God's plan.

ANNA: THE FAITHFUL WOMAN WITH AN UNYIELDING HEART

In Jesus' time, the Temple was the heart of the community. People visited the Temple during holidays, but it wasn't a place you'd go every day—unless you were Anna. An elderly woman who spent her days in the Temple, Anna had dedicated her life to God, living as a devout widow who relied on the community rather than worldly comforts.

Anna's constant presence at the Temple made her a familiar face, known to the priests and regular visitors. So when Mary and Joseph arrived with Jesus, Simeon recognized that Anna would understand the significance of the child.

Anna's reward for her devotion was to see the child who would fulfill God's promise. She teaches us that faithfulness has its own rewards, even if they don't come in the ways we expect.

HEROD: THE "GREAT" VILLAIN OF THE CHRISTMAS STORY

Every story needs a villain, and Herod fits the role perfectly. Known as "Herod the Great," he was ruthless, paranoid, and willing to eliminate anyone he saw as a threat to his power—even his own family.

Herod's rise to power began with his father, who had ties to Julius Caesar. Appointed as the governor of Galilee, Herod eventually became "King of the Jews," a title that fueled his paranoia and thirst for control. While he accomplished much in terms of architecture and governance—rebuilding the Temple, creating aqueducts, and establishing grand buildings—his cruelty overshadowed his achievements. Historians, like Josephus, described him as universally brutal, and on his deathbed, Herod famously ordered the deaths of prominent citizens to ensure mourning upon his passing.

Herod is remembered by Christians for his response to Jesus' birth. Although he claimed he wanted to worship the newborn king, his true intent was to eliminate any threat to his rule. This led to the "Massacre of the Innocents," where he ordered the killing of male infants in Bethlehem. His role in the Christmas story sets the stage for Jesus' family to flee to Egypt, mirroring Moses' story of deliverance from Egypt.

God's choice to lead Jesus and his family into Egypt serves as a profound symbol. Just as God led his people out of Egypt in the Old Covenant, in the New Covenant through Christ, he brings them back—signifying that this covenant is for all people, not just one nation.

ZECHARIAH: THE PRIESTLY FATHER

Zechariah, the father of John the Baptist, might seem like just another name in the Nativity story, but he's crucial for a few reasons. First, he's married to Elizabeth, and in a time when women were rarely mentioned, Elizabeth's role is highlighted. Luke's inclusion of Elizabeth points to a larger theme in his Gospel: women have an essential role in God's plan and the early church.

Zechariah himself was an elderly priest, likely in his sixties. His background gives us insight into John the Baptist's upbringing. Zechariah belonged to the tribe of Levi—the tribe designated for priests—meaning John was raised with a strong knowledge of Jewish laws and customs. As a priest, Zechariah had a once-in-a-lifetime chance to offer incense in the Temple when he encountered an angel with a message from God. This divine encounter shows us that, while Zechariah was a "man of God," he still had doubts. When the angel told him he and Elizabeth would have a child, Zechariah questioned how this could happen given their age. This moment reminds us that even the most faithful can struggle to believe.

Zechariah's faith, however, paved the way for John's life and mission. John would go on to prepare people for the message of Jesus, challenging old traditions and preparing hearts for the new message of salvation.

THE HEAVENLY MESSENGER

Angels hold a curious place in many people's beliefs—often, more people believe in angels than in God himself. While angels are real in the biblical sense, our modern view of them is often romanticized. We imagine them as gentle beings looking out for us, like our personal "guardian angels."

But the Bible gives us a different view. Angels are indeed "ministering spirits" sent to serve those who inherit salvation (Hebrews 1:14), and they are not to be worshipped (Revelation 22:8-9). Their purpose is not to receive our devotion or be our personal cheerleaders; they are messengers, sent to deliver God's instructions and protect when needed.

In the Nativity story, the angel Gabriel plays a central role, though the other angels may not be specifically named. Gabriel is known throughout the Bible as a protector and communicator, often delivering messages of great significance. In each instance of angelic intervention in the Christmas story, it's not the angel's presence that matters most, but the message they bring.

People often share stories about "car angels" who seemingly protect them from accidents or help in times of crisis. However, the focus on these stories is often on the angel's miraculous appearance rather than the divine will that sent them. In the Nativity story, the angels' purpose is clear: they come not to be admired but to reveal God's plan.

The lesson here is to focus on the message angels deliver, rather than on the angels themselves. Their role in the Christmas story is to communicate God's will—reminding us that it's God who guides, protects, and fulfills promises.

7

THE TOWN OF BETHLEHEM

For most of us, our birthplace doesn't hold any real weight. Being born in a particular city might earn us a birth certificate, but not much else. Bethlehem, however, was different for Jesus. Even though the town wasn't handing out perks to newborns, the city held deep significance, especially for a Jewish audience.

HISTORICAL BETHLEHEM

Bethlehem was a small town but packed with meaning. Its name, "house of bread," foreshadowed Jesus, who would be known as the "Bread of Life." Bethlehem was also the site where

Rachel, the beloved wife of Jacob, died, and it was the setting for the love story of Ruth and Boaz. Most importantly, it was the birthplace of King David, the figurehead of Jewish royalty.

To the Jewish people, Jesus' birth in Bethlehem fulfilled the prophecy that the Messiah would come from David's city. It hinted that Jesus, like David, would be a ruler. But while David led in the physical realm, Jesus would lead in the spiritual one, waging a battle for hearts and souls.

BETHLEHEM AT THE TIME OF JESUS' BIRTH

Knowing what Bethlehem was like when Jesus was born helps us see the Nativity story in a new light. When we imagine the scene, we often think of a "no room at the inn" moment and a humble manger, but understanding what these places were actually like in first-century Bethlehem adds depth to the story.

THE INN

We often picture an inn as a hotel with a front desk and "No Vacancy" sign. But in Jesus' day, inns were more like communal campgrounds. The closest equivalent to an "inn" was often a rough gathering spot for travelers, not the most comfortable or safe places.

The term "inn" can also be translated as "guest room," and many travelers stayed with relatives rather than in an actual inn. Given this, Mary and Joseph likely arrived at a family member's home only to find there was "no room" for them.

It's possible they weren't simply turned away because of a lack of space; they may have been shunned. The reality of Mary's pregnancy before marriage could have led some relatives to see her as a sinner, unworthy of a place in their home. While today's society might be more understanding, in Mary's time, such a situation could lead to outright rejection.

THE MANGER

With no room in the family's guest quarters, Mary and Joseph found themselves in the manger. But the "manger" might not have been a separate stable—it was likely a part of the family's home. Homes of that time often had an upper level for living quarters and a lower level for animals. It's possible that while the family didn't let them stay upstairs, they allowed Mary and Joseph to stay on the lower level with the animals.

This arrangement meant that Mary and Joseph had a roof over their heads, even if it wasn't ideal. And it also made the shepherds' search for Jesus easier, as they only had to look at homes with mangers.

The "manger story" isn't necessarily meant to evoke pity for Jesus' humble beginning. Instead, it reveals something about his parents —they were poor, humble, and relied on the kindness of others. From birth, Jesus' life was about community and interdependence. This experience likely influenced his later message that we are meant to support each other in a community of believers.

When Jesus grew up and heard the story of his birth, Mary and Joseph probably didn't recount it with bitterness. They likely spoke with gratitude for the help they received, even in difficult circumstances. These values of humility, gratitude, and love shaped the teachings Jesus would later share with the world. His birth story reminds us that life is better when we rely on each other and find strength in our community.

A HUMBLE DELIVERY ROOM FIT FOR A KING

Bethlehem's historical significance as the birthplace of a savior might seem like reason enough for Jesus to be born there. But if God's purpose was to mark Bethlehem as a royal birthplace, wouldn't the circumstances have been a bit more... royal? God could have ensured Mary had a comfortable bed, a private home, and the treatment fit for a king's birth.

Instead, he did the opposite.

Jesus was born in a place rich in history but stripped of any markers of wealth or status. God chose a humble setting to show that Jesus wasn't a king for the privileged or the powerful; he was a king for everyone. By placing Jesus in a manger, God made it clear that salvation is not about inheritance, wealth, or accomplishments. Salvation is a gift—freely given and accessible to anyone who accepts it.

But the significance of Jesus' birth in Bethlehem doesn't end there. Shortly after, Joseph takes his family to Egypt, establishing a powerful parallel with the story of Moses.

FROM BETHLEHEM TO EGYPT: PARALLELS WITH MOSES

The Nativity story echoes the story of Moses but in reverse. Moses was born in Egypt, and God led his people out of Egypt to Israel, forming a covenant with them in the Promised Land. In contrast, Jesus was born in Israel, and out of danger, God led him to Egypt. This movement symbolically brings the people back to where the journey started, hinting at a new covenant that will be open to everyone.

God could have prevented Herod's cruel decree, but he allowed Jesus' family to flee, showing that Jesus' mission would extend beyond Israel. By setting the stage in Bethlehem—a city rich in Jewish symbolism—and then directing them to Egypt, God sent a clear message: Jesus wasn't going to be just the king of Israel; he was going to be the king for all people, including the Gentiles.

Through Jesus' humble birth in Bethlehem and his journey to Egypt, God declared that the Savior of the world wouldn't be limited to a single nation or group. Instead, he would be a Savior for all humanity.

8

STAR OF BETHLEHEM

In a place like Southern California, stars are rare sights. City lights overpower them, making stargazing a luxury that requires miles of travel away from the city. But out in the desert, where the night sky is clearer, stars fill the heavens—a sight that brings to mind the Nativity Star. What made that star so unique? Was it some grand, miraculous spectacle, or was it something more subtle?

THE BIBLICAL STAR

The Bible's account of the Nativity Star might surprise you with its simplicity. We often picture it as an otherworldly beacon, but in

Matthew 2:2, we find a straightforward statement:

"Where is the one who has been born king of the Jews? We saw his star when it rose and have come to worship him." (NIV)

Later, in verse 9, we read:

"After they had heard the king, they went on their way, and the star they had seen when it rose went ahead of them until it stopped over the place where the child was." (NIV)

The star appears to guide the Wise Men, but it wasn't necessarily a blazing light hovering over the manger as we often imagine. Instead, it was simply enough to direct the Wise Men on their path.

THE SCIENTIFIC STAR

Science has its own theories about the Star, proposing that it might have been anything from a meteor to Halley's Comet. But a star bright enough to guide people usually leaves records from various cultures, and in this case, not all regions noted anything unusual. The star seems to have been visible only in a specific area.

Why would God choose a star that wasn't seen by everyone? God rarely draws people to him through overwhelming force or spectacle. He allows us to come to him naturally, with subtle signs that invite, not compel. The Star was a quiet but powerful message—a guiding light for those who were paying attention.

CHRISTMAS LIGHTS: A MODERN STAR

Growing up, one of the Christmas traditions was visiting a neighborhood fully decked out in holiday lights, known as Candy Cane Lane. Each house was decorated with care, with neighbors coming together to ensure even the most reluctant got into the spirit. The lights were a beautiful display, symbolizing Christmas joy, but perhaps they carried an even deeper meaning.

In those Christmas lights, we can see a reflection of the Nativity Star. They're a reminder of the light that guided the Wise Men and of the light Jesus brought into the world. In Genesis, God spoke light into existence, and in John's Gospel, that light took on new meaning:

"In the beginning was the Word, and the Word was with God, and the Word was God… In him was life, and that life was the light of all mankind. The light shines in the darkness, and the darkness has not overcome it." (John 1:1-5, NIV)

While John doesn't mention the Star itself, he speaks of Jesus as the light that entered the world. It's no coincidence that a star marked Jesus' birth and darkness covered the land when he died:

"From noon until three in the afternoon darkness came over all the land." (Matthew 27:45, NIV)

The light that entered the world with Jesus' birth was extinguished as he took on the sins of the world. Through these symbolic moments, God illustrated Jesus' journey—entering the world as a guiding light and leaving it in darkness to save humanity.

GOD DOESN'T OFTEN REVEAL himself through spectacle or flashy displays. He speaks through symbols and acts, inviting us to see the deeper meaning. The Nativity Star wasn't just a miraculous sign—it was a reminder that light had come into the world, bringing hope and guidance to all who looked for it.

So the next time you admire Christmas lights, let them remind you of that light. Let them symbolize the presence of God, who entered the world quietly, with an invitation to all. Remember that those lights, however simple or secular their setting, hold a message: the Word became flesh, and the light of Christmas continues to shine in the darkness.

9

THE SHEPHERDS

How often do we hear sermons about the shepherds in the Nativity story? Probably not as often as the Wise Men. In fact, you might even be wondering, "Weren't the Wise Men and shepherds the same?" The shepherds are a bit of a mystery; they're part of the story, but their role feels understated. They don't bring gifts from faraway lands or come with fanfare. Their only gift is their presence. But as with every detail in the Bible, there's more here than meets the eye.

THE BIBLICAL SHEPHERDS

Let's start with the biblical account in Luke 2:8-20. The shepherds were out in the fields at night when an angel appeared to them, delivering the news of Jesus' birth:

"And there were shepherds living out in the fields nearby, keeping watch over their flocks at night... But the angel said to them, 'Do not be afraid. I bring you good news that will cause great joy for all the people. Today in the town of David a Savior has been born to you; he is the Messiah, the Lord...'" (NIV)

At first, the shepherds are terrified—a typical reaction in the Bible when encountering God or his messengers. In the Old Testament, the relationship between God and humanity was one of separation due to sin. The idea of a "personal" God wasn't common. But here, the angel tells the shepherds not to fear; this news is about bridging that gap. The birth of Jesus represents the start of a New Covenant, one based on closeness rather than separation.

When the shepherds leave, they're no longer afraid. They're filled with joy and praise, understanding that this child represents something new—a God who is close, a God they can approach.

WHO WERE THE SHEPHERDS?

To understand why God chose the shepherds, we need to know a bit about what it meant to be a shepherd. Shepherds weren't city folk; they were outsiders, living on the edges of society, working a job that was hard and thankless. They stayed up in shifts to guard their sheep from predators and thieves, often sleeping under the stars.

Despite their important role, especially during Passover when lambs were needed for sacrifices, shepherds themselves were considered unclean. They weren't welcomed in the temple. Society's attitude toward shepherds was often a "we need you, but we don't want you around" kind of deal—a sentiment that might sound familiar even today.

For the readers of Luke, the message is clear: this savior isn't just for the elite or religiously pure. He's for everyone, including those on the margins. Christ is coming for the outsiders, like the shepherds, who are a symbol of humility and service.

There's also a layer of irony in the shepherds' story. On the night they visit Jesus, they're seeing the end of their own role. Jesus, as the ultimate "Lamb of God," will replace the need for sacrificial lambs. The shepherds witness the very one who will fulfill and transform the purpose of their work. They realize there is something greater than themselves, something worth celebrating, even if it means the end of their job.

THE SHEPHERDS' MESSAGE

The shepherds saw in Jesus a promise of something more—something worth humbling themselves for. They were willing to accept that this newborn represented a shift in what mattered. The Christmas story is a call to humility, a reminder that it's not about our old identities, our roles, or the material things we cling to. It's about something greater: the light and hope brought into the world by that child in the manger.

When we think of Christmas, it's easy to

focus on family traditions, gifts, and decorations. But the true message is in the shepherds' story—a story of people who saw that in Christ, there was something worth giving up everything for. This season, let the shepherds remind us that Christmas is about humbling ourselves, recognizing the greatness of what God has given, and letting go of our old selves to embrace something far greater.

10

THE WISE MEN

When a baby is born, visits from family and friends are expected. But for Jesus, the only visitors mentioned in the Bible are the Wise Men, also known as the Magi. It's easy to wonder why they're included at all—were they simply wise, or did they bring something special to the story? Though the Magi play a brief and somewhat mysterious role in Matthew's Gospel, their presence carries deep meaning, and they are far more important than they first appear.

Interestingly, many Nativity scenes and pageants show the Wise Men arriving at the manger, bearing gifts on camels. But the Bible doesn't actually describe it that way. In fact, these Magi most likely arrived much later, visiting Jesus not as an infant in a manger, but as a young child in a house. The traditional scene we know is more about artistic license than biblical accuracy.

THE BIBLICAL ACCOUNT OF THE WISE MEN

The Magi's story appears only in the Gospel of Matthew (Matthew 2:1-12):

"After Jesus was born in Bethlehem...Magi from the east came to Jerusalem and asked, 'Where is the one who has been born king of the Jews? We saw his star when it rose and have come to worship him.'" (NIV)

When King Herod hears of this "king," he's disturbed. Known for his paranoia and ruthless grip on power, Herod was just the type of person to eliminate anyone he saw as a threat. The Magi continue on their journey, guided by the star, and finally find Jesus, presenting him with gifts of gold, frankincense, and myrrh. But after being warned in a dream, they avoid

Herod on their return, knowing his intentions are anything but friendly.

WHO WERE THE WISE MEN?

Contrary to popular belief, the Bible never states that there were three Wise Men—only that there were multiple men bringing three gifts. The number three likely stuck because it's simpler for art and storytelling. The term "Magi" itself is also somewhat mysterious; Magi appeared in various roles across cultures, often as priests, advisors, or even interpreters of dreams. We don't know where exactly they came from, but they were likely foreigners, not of Jewish origin, who traveled from the East— likely Persia or Babylon, regions where Magi were known.

The Magi were probably part of a larger caravan with servants and guards, as traveling alone in those days was both impractical and dangerous. The Bible implies they arrived at a house rather than a stable, and Jesus was likely a toddler by then. It's possible they witnessed something extraordinary about the child that made them fall down in worship, despite not fully understanding his significance within Jewish prophecy.

WHAT DO THE WISE MEN REPRESENT?

The Wise Men's gifts—gold, frankincense, and myrrh—each carry symbolic meaning, representing Jesus as king (gold), priest (frankincense), and the sacrifice he would become (myrrh). But their presence in the story represents something more: the idea that Jesus is not just for Israel, but for all people. These foreign visitors recognize Jesus' significance and come to honor him, signifying the global reach of his impact and the universality of his message.

The Wise Men didn't need a star to guide them, being experienced travelers, but the star marked something important: a light for those who are searching. Their journey, their gifts, and their reverence show that they saw in Jesus something worth traveling miles to honor.

So while the Magi might seem like minor figures, they are in fact pivotal. They bridge cultures and symbolize the far-reaching hope that Jesus brings. This Christmas, the story of the Wise Men reminds us that Jesus came for everyone, near and far, and that his light shines for those who seek it, no matter where they come from.

WHY THE WISE MEN?

Why did the Wise Men need to see Jesus? Their journey represents a major turning point in the story of God and humanity. They weren't Jews; they were learned men from a distant land, unfamiliar with the teachings of Judaism. Through their journey, God was signaling something profound: *I'm here for everyone—not just the Jews, but all people.*

The Wise Men also provide a lesson about belief. Herod "believed" that Jesus was a special child, but he viewed him as a threat and wanted him dead. Just knowing who Jesus is doesn't mean having a relationship with him. The Wise Men model what a true relationship with Christ should look like:

1. **They sought truth:** The Magi were on a quest to know something deeper. Despite being wise and learned, they continued to search

for more. We all have a sense of wonder and spiritual curiosity within us, and like the Magi, we should follow it.

2. **They obeyed:** The Wise Men didn't wait for the "right time." Despite the risks and Herod's reputation, they went to see Jesus. They trusted in a higher purpose.

3. **They worshiped:** When they saw Jesus, they recognized his significance. Worship here might mean different things, from honoring him as royalty to experiencing a sense of divinity. Whatever the case, they saw something in Jesus beyond the ordinary.

4. **They gave thanks:** Their gifts symbolized their respect and reverence, giving Jesus their best.

WHAT DOES IT MEAN THAT THEY WORSHIPED?

The Wise Men worshiped Jesus, but this could have been more about reverence than the worship we think of today. In their culture, "worship" could mean acknowledging someone's importance or status. But if they saw Jesus as divine, this moment would have changed them, influencing what they did next and possibly transforming their lives.

WHAT HAPPENED TO THE WISE MEN?

The Wise Men come into the story as mysteriously as they leave. After their encounter with Jesus, did they go back to their regular lives? Or did this experience change them?

One theory, proposed by Dwight Longenecker in *Mystery of the Magi*, suggests that the Wise Men may have settled in Damascus, opening a school of wisdom. Interestingly, Paul, who played a significant role in spreading Christianity to the Gentiles, spent time in Damascus after his conversion. If Paul studied with the Wise Men, it could explain why he was so adept at relating the gospel to non-Jewish audiences. He understood how to speak to different cultures, making connections between their beliefs and the message of Christ.

If the Wise Men truly saw Jesus as divine, it's likely they went back changed, perhaps living lives of simplicity rather than wealth. We don't know for certain, but the idea that they shared their wisdom and influenced Paul's teachings is compelling. It would mean their encounter with Jesus had a ripple effect, helping spread his message far beyond Israel.

MORE THAN MEETS THE EYE?

Could the Wise Men have impacted Jesus' ministry directly? It's possible, though speculative. Damascus wasn't far from where Jesus grew up, and there is a long gap between Jesus' childhood and the beginning of his ministry. Perhaps Jesus learned about the Gentiles and other cultures from someone well-versed in them.

Whether or not the Wise Men were Jesus' direct teachers, their journey demonstrates that God's message reaches far beyond borders, cultures, and religions. Their role in the Nativity is more than symbolic—they are a reminder that faith isn't confined to one group. Jesus came for everyone, and the Wise Men's visit sets the stage for a message that would ultimately reach every corner of the world.

11

THE GIFTS

The Wise Men are perhaps most famous for the gifts they brought: gold, frankincense, and myrrh. We hear about these gifts so often that they seem normal, but if we pause and think, they're actually quite unusual. When most people have a baby, they receive practical items—baby clothes, blankets, maybe even a gift card. Not many people gift gold, frankincense, or myrrh for a newborn. So, were these Wise Men terrible gift-givers, or is there more to these gifts?

THE GIFTS AT FACE VALUE

The Bible is often layered with symbolism, and these gifts are no exception. But before we dive into possible symbolic meanings, we should look at the cultural context. Gold, frankincense, and myrrh were all valuable Middle Eastern commodities.

- **Gold** was then, as now, a universal sign of wealth and value.
- **Myrrh** was a natural pain reliever and was often used on battlefields; it's notable that it was offered to Jesus during the crucifixion, though he declined it.
- **Frankincense** was used medicinally to reduce inflammation and was often part of temple worship.

To Matthew's readers, these gifts would have represented some of the most valuable items one could bring. They were gifts suited to royalty, showing respect and honor. Additionally, these valuable gifts likely provided Joseph and Mary with the resources needed for their sudden flight to Egypt—a journey neither short nor inexpensive in those times.

GIFTS AS SYMBOLS

The gifts weren't just practical; they carried symbolic weight:

- **Gold** represents Jesus' kingship, acknowledging his rule on Earth.
- **Frankincense**, often used in religious rituals, could symbolize Jesus' priestly role, anointing him for a holy mission.
- **Myrrh**, used for embalming, hints at the suffering and sacrifice Jesus would endure.

While these symbolic interpretations are thought-provoking, it's essential to remember that the Wise Men were likely honoring Jesus with the best treasures they had, gifts reserved for kings and royalty.

CHRISTMAS' TRUE GIFT

When we think about Christmas gifts, we often reflect on what we give each other. The

Magi's gifts to Jesus might add some depth to the Christmas story, but they shouldn't overshadow the true gift of Christmas.

Isaiah 9:6 says, "For to us a child is born, to us a son is given." The greatest gift is not the gold, frankincense, or myrrh, but what God gave to us: Jesus himself. He was more than a baby in a manger; he was—and is—the gift of salvation.

As we exchange presents this season, let's remember the ultimate gift, a gift given to all of humanity—Jesus, the true King. This is the gift that defines Christmas, reminding us that God's love is freely given, just waiting for us to accept.

EPILOGUE

Christmas is a time for celebration, a season filled with traditions, memories, and meaning that vary from family to family. For my family, it was the little things—like finding a banana in our stockings every year. This quirky tradition, started to make our stockings look full, became a beloved memory. As adults, my brother and I would still look for that banana, feeling disappointed if it wasn't there. Simple as it was, it was a reminder of tradition, comfort, and home.

Christmas isn't about the value of the gifts as much as it is about having something to look forward to. For children, there's a sense of wonder and anticipation—sometimes around a magical figure named Santa, but that wonder also hints at something deeper. In many ways, Santa becomes symbolic of the surprise and joy Christ brings. Imagine if we, as adults, could hold onto that same innocent awe for Christmas—that would be a miracle.

Throughout his life, Jesus called us to return to the state of being like children. He wasn't telling us to act immaturely, but to regain the innocence and openness of a child —to live without fear and to trust deeply, knowing we are cared for. Children live in the present, not burdened by yesterday or tomorrow. They feel secure, held by the love of their parents. Jesus came as a child to remind us of that state, to show us the beauty of innocence and dependence on God.

SEEING THE NATIVITY ANEW

Understanding the real Nativity story isn't about unraveling all we learned in childhood but about seeing its deeper layers. God could have appeared to us as a fully grown man, but he chose to come as a child. This was to remind us that true faith means embracing the openness and trust of a child's heart.

Christmas has become saturated with sayings like, "You can't have Christmas without Christ." While true, it doesn't capture the full, rich spirit of the season. The Bible's version of Christmas is more profound and spiritual than our modern take—it shows us joy, worship, and God's unexpected ways of reaching us. True Christmas can't be wrapped in paper; it's wrapped in love, shared with the world through our actions.

A TRADITION OF LOVE

Paul, who may have been influenced by teachings similar to the Wise Men's, was an expert in living within the world while using it to share God's love. Every tradition, every celebration can be an opportunity to glorify God—even our Christmas customs. Just as the early church took Winter Solstice traditions and infused them with Christian meaning, we, too, can keep our traditions but let them point back to the heart of the Nativity story.

This Christmas, think about a tradition that

helps your family celebrate the true meaning of Christ's birth. Make room to honor God in ways that bring love, wonder, and joy into the world. This is the real gift of Christmas, a legacy of love that began that night in Bethlehem and continues each time we share that love with others.

APPENDIX A: ADVENT

Advent season is prime time for churches. As the holiday nears, families begin crowding in, watching candles being lit while many might be thinking more about the brunch buffet afterward than the significance of the season itself. If you ask the average person about Advent, they'd likely say, "Oh, it's what we do before Christmas!"—but if you follow up with, "Yeah, but why?" they'd probably just shrug.

The truth is, Advent is to Christmas what Lent is to Easter. It's a time of preparation, even if few people can fully explain its origins or significance. Here's a quick overview.

THE HISTORY OF ADVENT: SIMPLE BUT MYSTERIOUS

Advent's purpose is to prepare us for Christmas, but its historical roots are not all that clear. Though its official origins are uncertain, it's believed that around 500 AD, church leaders introduced Advent as a time of spiritual preparation for Christmas. The Council of Tours in 567 even went so far as to declare Advent a time of reflection and mandated that monks and priests observe it.

It's a simple holiday that isn't bogged down with theological complications or obscure symbolism. Instead, it's a time to prepare our hearts to celebrate God's gift. That preparation means reflecting on what Christ's birth means for us, spiritually and relationally.

PREPARING OUR HEARTS FOR CHRISTMAS

Advent encourages us to think about Christmas not as a time of frantic shopping or fancy meals but as a spiritual season where we focus on the real gift—Christ himself. Advent

Appendix A: Advent

asks us to look within, to consider how Christ's arrival changed everything, and to think about how it impacts our lives and our relationships.

Imagine spending the weeks leading up to Christmas with a daily reminder of this devotion. Rather than just planning the material festivities, take some time to pray, reflect, and think about where you'd be without the gift of Christ. You might find yourself celebrating Christmas in a deeper, more meaningful way than ever before.

APPENDIX B: HISTORY OF CHRISTMAS

The Nativity story may be familiar, but Christmas as we know it today—with trees, mistletoe, and gift-giving—took centuries to evolve. Contrary to what some might think, Christmas didn't start right after Jesus' birth, nor even directly after his death; in fact, it only developed several hundred years later and has undergone many transformations since then.

Here's a look at the intriguing—and sometimes unexpected—history of Christmas.

THE ORIGIN OF GIFT-GIVING

Gift-giving is central to Christmas today, but how did it become a tradition? While it's tempting to trace it back to the Magi bringing gifts to Jesus, the practice didn't actually begin this way. Gift-giving in winter dates back to Roman times when people exchanged presents around New Year's. As Christianity spread, this practice shifted to align with the celebration of Jesus' birth, taking on new meaning.

But the way we recognize Christmas gift-giving today can largely be credited to New York City in the 1800s. During that time, the holiday was associated with public celebrations that often got a bit out of hand, with drunken revelries filling the streets. New Yorkers, eager to curb the raucous nature of the festivities, began promoting the idea of a family-centered Christmas celebrated at home. Stores like Macy's soon began displaying toys, creating a tradition of buying gifts—one that would only grow more commercial over time.

SANTA CLAUS: A LEGENDARY TRANSFORMATION

The folklore surrounding Santa Claus is the stuff of legend—stories of St. Nicholas abound, and interpretations vary widely. Historically, St.

Appendix B: History of Christmas 97

Nicholas, who lived around 280 AD in what is now Turkey, is thought to have been a wealthy man who used his fortune to help the needy. Some say he became a monk, while others believe he held the title of Bishop of Myra, possibly even attending the Council of Nicaea.

But the idea of Santa Claus goes beyond St. Nicholas. European traditions from various countries, including Germany's Yule celebrations, each have their own versions of a bearded, gift-giving figure. This figure eventually evolved into the Santa Claus we recognize today, thanks in part to the 1823 poem *A Visit from St. Nicholas*, which painted a picture of a jolly man in a sleigh. Later in the 19th century, James Edgar, a department store owner, dressed up as Santa and walked the streets, spreading Christmas cheer—a tradition that solidified Santa's place in department stores and holiday traditions.

CHRISTMAS: BANNED AND REBORN

Though it might surprise many, Christmas was once banned by Christians who saw it as a time of excessive indulgence. During the Protestant

Reformation, church leaders condemned the holiday's pagan roots and drunken celebrations, even pushing for an official ban in England in 1647. Christmas revelries continued in secret, but it wasn't until 1681, under Charles II, that Christmas was once again openly celebrated.

Interestingly, Puritans in the early American colonies shared this disapproval, leading some Christians to emphasize the holiday's secular aspects. This shift is partly why Christmas today has such strong secular associations—a twist of irony given the Puritans' intentions.

A ROYAL REVIVAL

The real revival of Christmas can be traced to Queen Victoria and Prince Albert, who brought German Christmas traditions, including the Christmas tree, to England's royal family in the mid-1800s. Once British newspapers published images of the royal family celebrating around a tree, the tradition caught on across England.

In the United States, Christmas only

became a federal holiday in 1870, cementing its place in American culture largely thanks to the influence of German immigrants and department stores.

Christmas is a blend of influences—ancient and modern, secular and sacred—that together create the holiday we celebrate today. From gift-giving and Santa Claus to decorated trees and family gatherings, each element has its own rich, sometimes surprising, backstory that adds depth to our holiday traditions.

Milton Keynes UK
Ingram Content Group UK Ltd.
UKHW020028271124
451585UK00014B/1523